I0821458

My First Look at Simple Machines
Screws
Katie Marsico
LIGHTBOX
openlightbox.com

Lightbox is an all-inclusive digital solution for the teaching and learning of curriculum topics in an original, groundbreaking way. Lightbox is based on National Curriculum Standards.

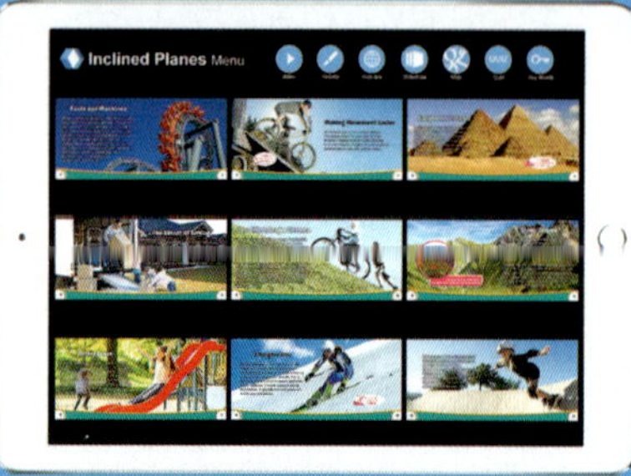

OPTIMIZED FOR

- ✓ TABLETS
- ✓ WHITEBOARDS
- ✓ COMPUTERS
- ✓ AND MUCH MORE!

STANDARD FEATURES OF LIGHTBOX

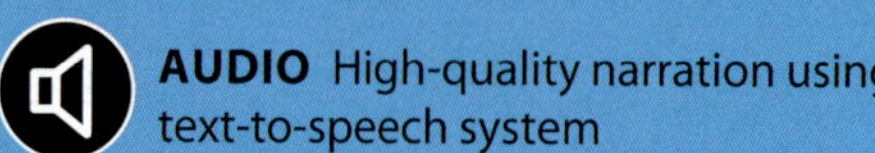
AUDIO High-quality narration using text-to-speech system

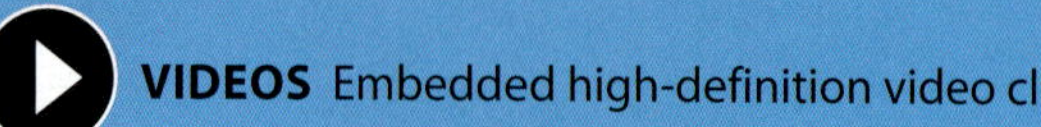
VIDEOS Embedded high-definition video clips

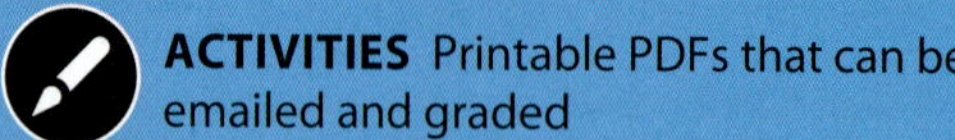
ACTIVITIES Printable PDFs that can be emailed and graded

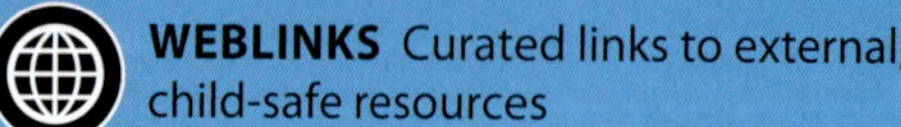
WEBLINKS Curated links to external, child-safe resources

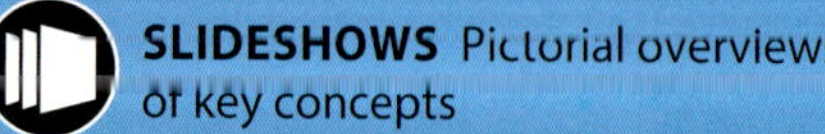
SLIDESHOWS Pictorial overviews of key concepts

INTERACTIVE MAPS Interactive maps and aerial satellite imagery

QUIZZES Ten multiple choice questions that are automatically graded and emailed for teacher assessment

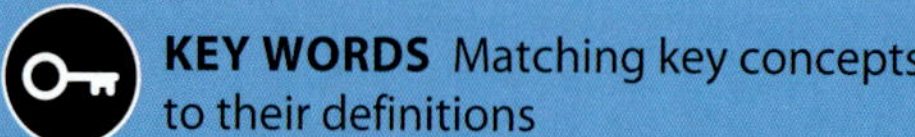
KEY WORDS Matching key concepts to their definitions

VIDEOS

WEBLINKS

SLIDESHOWS

QUIZZES

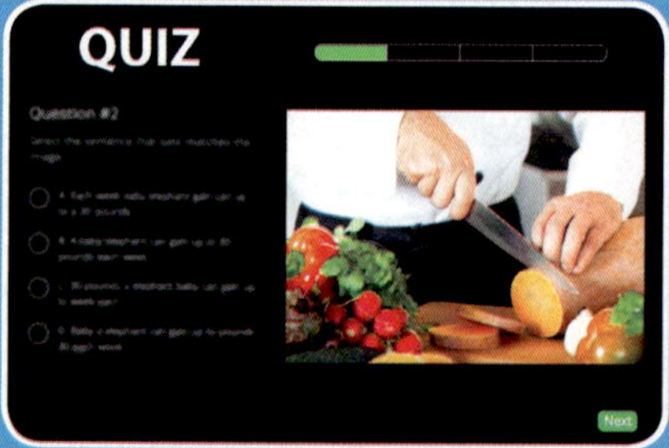

My First Look at Simple Machines

Screws

Contents

Tools and Machines

What would your life be like without tools and machines? You use tools and machines every day. Tools and machines help you work. Computers are machines Cars are machines, too. Washing machines help you clean your clothes. These machines have many moving parts. They are made up of many simple machines. There are six types of simple machines. It's time to learn about screws. Let's get to work!

A **scissor car jack** uses a **screw**. This lets **one person** lift up the side of a car to replace a tire.

A Kind of Ramp

An inclined plane is usually just a straight, slanted surface connecting two different levels. Think of a slide on the playground. A screw is different, though. A screw's ramp is wrapped around a tube. Screws help lock things together. They can hold heavy things up, too.

Parts of a Screw

Screws have three parts. The head is on top. The cylinder is the long middle. The point is the end. The thread is the inclined plane part. The thread wraps around the cylinder.

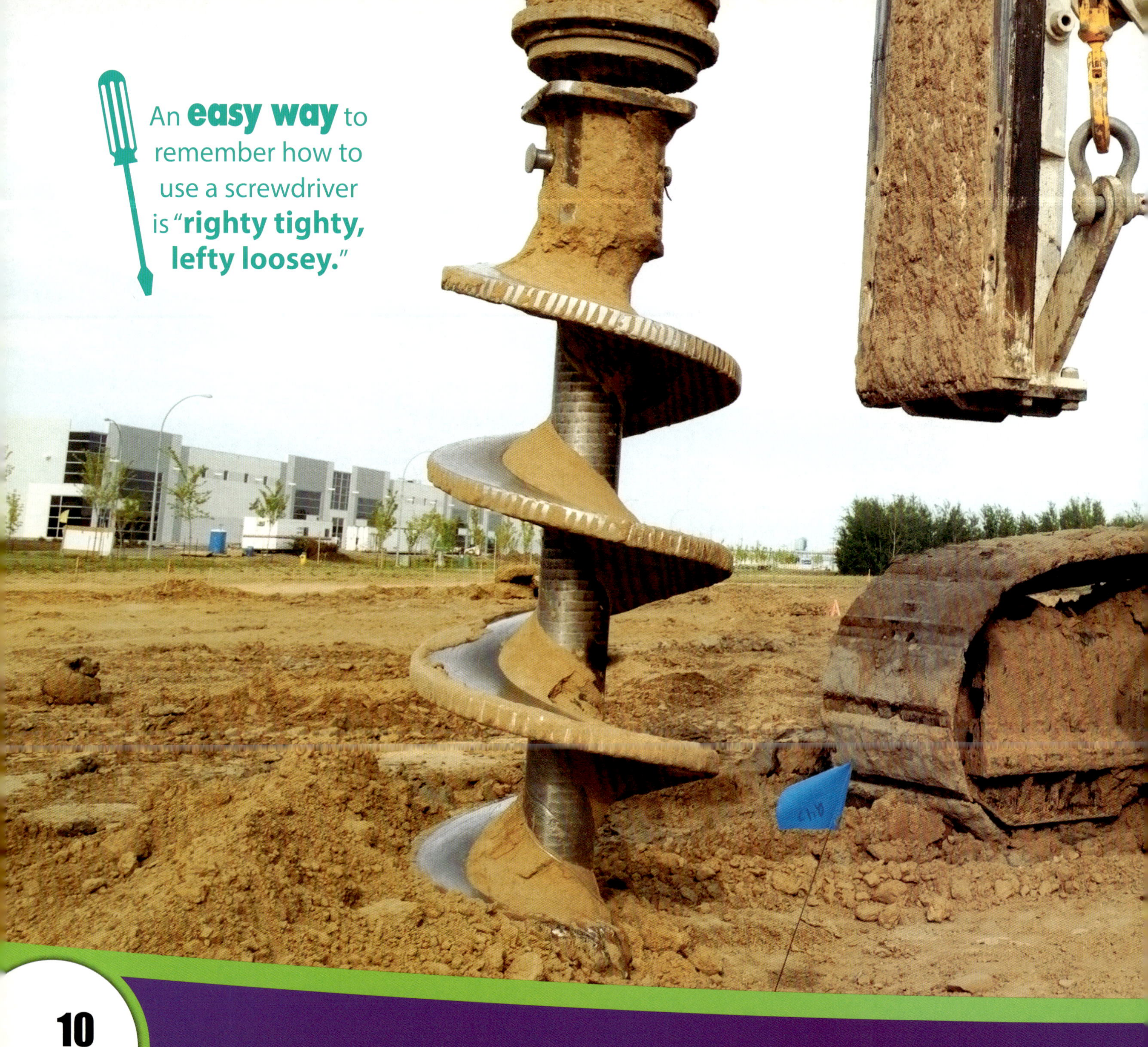

An **easy way** to remember how to use a screwdriver is "**righty tighty, lefty loosey.**"

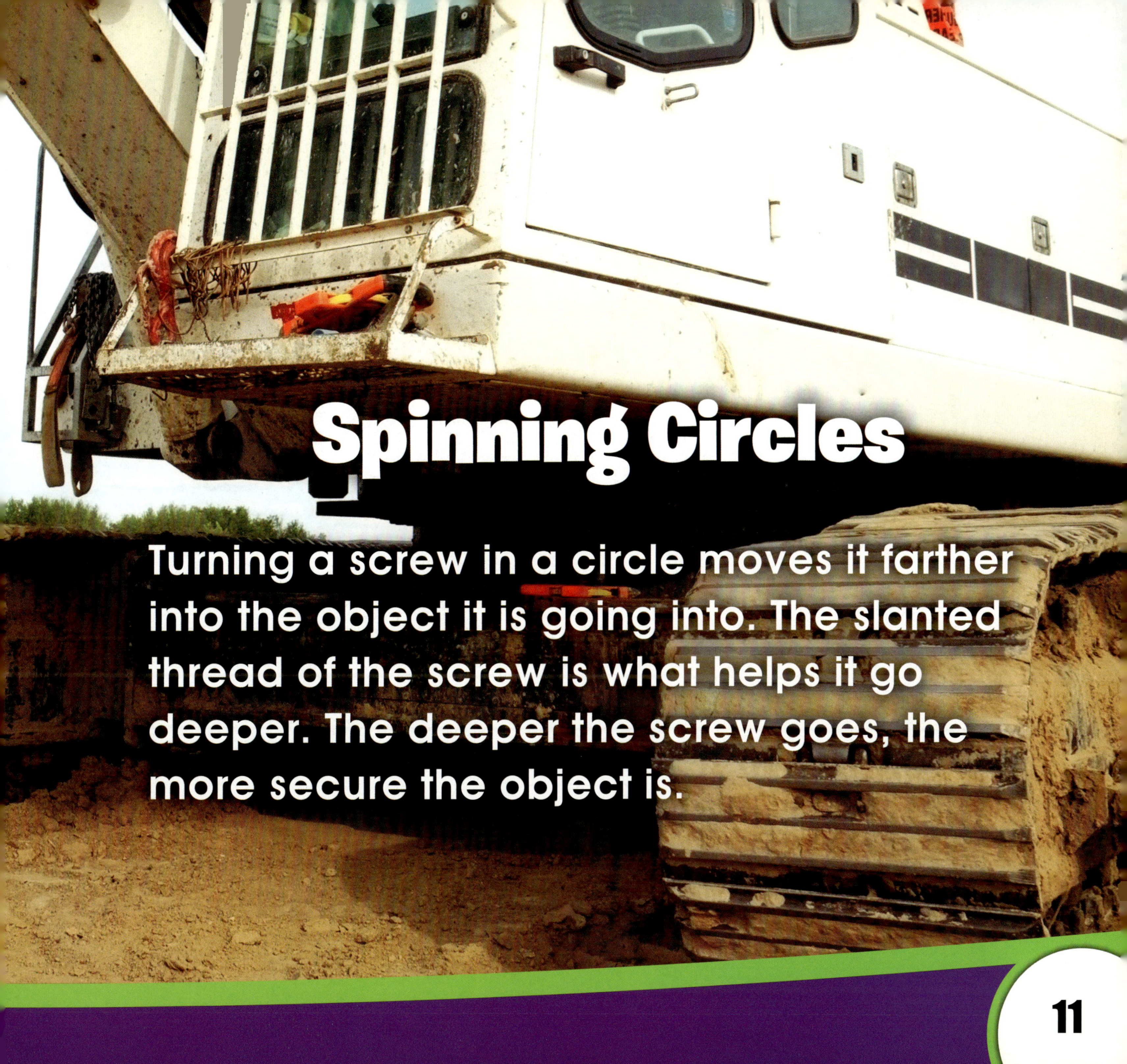

Spinning Circles

Turning a screw in a circle moves it farther into the object it is going into. The slanted thread of the screw is what helps it go deeper. The deeper the screw goes, the more secure the object is.

Thread Power

A screw's thread is what gives the screw power. The thread helps hold things better than a nail. A nail has a straight cylinder without a thread. A nail goes deep. But it will not be as secure as a screw because its cylinder is smooth.

Imagine you have a heavy picture to hang on the wall. Do you think a nail or a screw will hold it better? A screw, of course!

An **Archimedes screw** moves **water** from one place to another.

Pitch

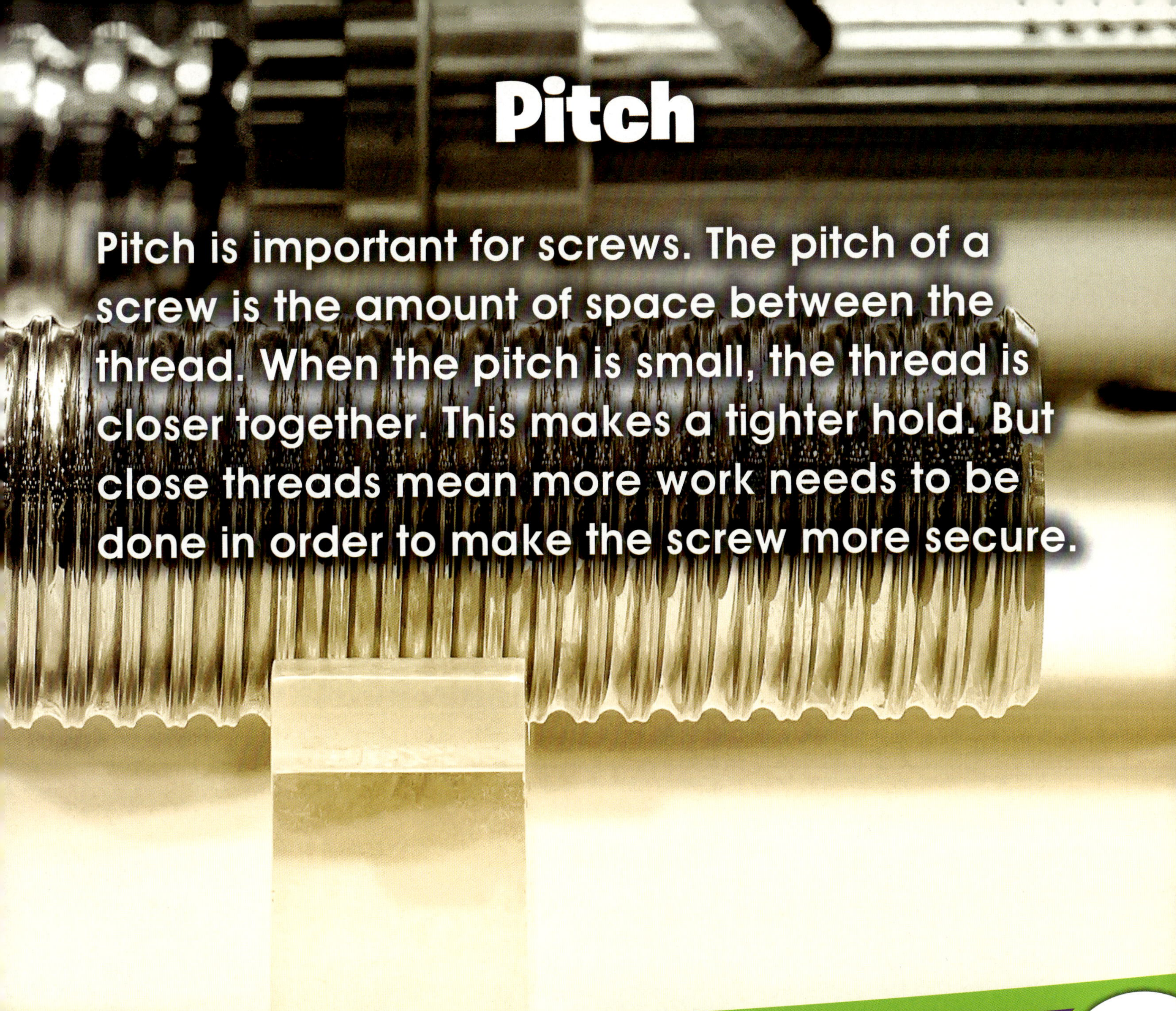

Pitch is important for screws. The pitch of a screw is the amount of space between the thread. When the pitch is small, the thread is closer together. This makes a tighter hold. But close threads mean more work needs to be done in order to make the screw more secure.

Screws and Bolts

Screws are related to bolts. Bolts have threads, too. Screws and bolts help keep objects locked together. However, screws can be used by themselves. Bolts are used with other pieces called nuts to hold things together.

The world's largest light bulb is on the Thomas Edison Memorial Tower in Edison, New Jersey.

Do you have jars in your cabinets or refrigerator? Look on the top edge of a jar. Do you see the thread? When you turn the lid on your jam jar, the thread helps the lid get nice and tight.

Have you ever changed a light bulb? If so, you would have seen a screw on it. The screw tightens the light bulb into place so you can have a bright room for reading.

In Complex Machines

Screws are used in many complex machines to keep parts together. You can find screws in cars, farming equipment, and computers. Wherever two objects need to be locked together on a machine, you will probably find a screw.

Screws Everywhere

Now you know about screws. These simple machines are everywhere! They are behind your family portrait on the wall. They are inside lamps. Where else in your home can you find screws?

KEY WORDS

Research has shown that as much as 65 percent of all written material published in English is made up of 300 words. These 300 words cannot be taught using pictures or learned by sounding them out. They must be recognized by sight. This book contains 101 common sight words to help young readers improve their reading fluency and comprehension. This book also teaches young readers several important content words, such as proper nouns. These words are paired with pictures to aid in learning and improve understanding.

Page	Sight Words First Appearance
4	about, and, are, be, cars, day, every, get, have, help, it's, learn, life, like, made, many, of, parts, there, these, they, time, to, too, up, use, what, without, work, would, you, your
6	lets, one, side, this
7	an, around, can, different, is, just, kind, on, the, things, think, together, two
8	end, head, long, point, three
10	how, way
11	go, in, into, it, more, moves
12	as, because, but, do, gives, has, its, not, or, picture, than, will
14	another, from, place, water
15	between, for, important, makes, mean, needs, small
16	by, keep, other, with
18	world
19	if, look, see, so, turn
20	find
23	family, home, know, now, where

Page	Content Words First Appearance
4	clothes, computers, machines, screws, tools, washing machines
6	car jack, person, tire
7	inclined plane, levels, playground, ramp, slide, tube
8	cylinder, middle, thread, top
10	screwdriver
11	circles
12	nail, wall
14	Archimedes Screw
15	pitch, space
16	bolts, nuts
18	Edison, New Jersey, light bulb
19	cabinets, refrigerator
20	farming equipment
23	lamps

Published by Smartbook Media Inc.
350 5th Avenue, 59th Floor New York, NY 10118
Website: www.openlightbox.com

Library of Congress Control Number: 2016957924

ISBN 978-1-5105-2067-7 (hardcover)
ISBN 978-1-5105-2068-4 (multi-user eBook)

Printed in the United States of America in Brainerd, Minnesota
1 2 3 4 5 6 7 8 9 0 20 19 18 17 16

122016
122216

Project Coordinator: Piper Whelan
Designer: Ana María Vidal

Every reasonable effort has been made to trace ownership and to obtain permission to reprint copyright material. The publisher would be pleased to have any errors or omissions brought to its attention so that they may be corrected in subsequent printings.

The publisher acknowledges Alamy, iStock, Getty Images, and Shutterstock as the primary image suppliers for this title.